How to Do Things
with Tears

ALSO BY ALLEN GROSSMAN

POETRY

A Harlot's Hire (1961)

The Recluse (1965)

And the Dew Lay All Night Upon My Branch (1973)

The Woman on the Bridge Over the Chicago River (1979)

Of the Great House: A Book of Poems (1982)

The Bright Nails Scattered on the Ground (1986)

The Ether Dome & Other Poems New & Selected (1979–1991) (1991)

The Philosopher's Window and Other Poems (1995)

The Song of the Lord. An audio tape on which the author
reads poems selected from *The Ether Dome,*
published by Watershed Tapes.

PROSE

The Long Schoolroom: Lessons in the Bitter Logic of the Poetic (1997)

Poetic Knowledge in Early Yeats (1970)

The Sighted Singer: Two Works on Poetry for Readers and Writers,
with Mark Halliday (1991). Revised and augmented edition
containing *Against Our Vanishing: Winter and Summer Coversations
on the Theory and Practice of Poetry* (1980, 1990) and *Summa Lyrica:
A Primer of the Commonplace in Speculative Poetics*

How to Do Things with Tears

By Allen Grossman

A NEW DIRECTIONS BOOK

Copyright © 2001 by Allen Grossman

ACKNOWLEDGMENTS

Prior publication of certain of the poems in this book: "How to do things with tears" in *Yale Review*, "Enough rain for Agnes Walquist" in *Southern Review*, "Truluv the sailor" in *Chicago Review*, "Epistola" in *Common Knowledge*, "Weird River" in *Partisan Review*, "Flora's ABC" in *Antioch Review*, "SHAZAM!" in *Boston Review*, "Latch" in *Ploughshares*, "A Grand Caprice" in *Fence*, "X-rated" in *TriQuarterly*, "Your laughing lover" in *Image*, "Crow" in *Saltbox*, "Star Asper" in *Boulevard*.

Book design by Sylvia Frezzolini Severance
Manufactured in the United States of America
New Directions Books are published on acid-free paper.
First published as New Directions Paperbook 912 in 2001
Published simultaneously in Canada by Penguin Books Canada Limited

Library of Congress Cataloging-in-Publication Data

Grossman, Allen R., 1932–
How to do things with tears / by Allen Grossman.
    p. cm. — (New Directions paperbook; 912)
Poems.
ISBN 0–8112–1464–8 (alk. paper)
    I. Title

PS3557.R67 H69 2001
811'.54—dc21
                                                    00-050093

New Directions Books are published for James Laughlin
by New Directions Publishing Corporation,
80 Eighth Avenue, New York, NY 10011

Contents

What these poems undertake to do   xii

Part One HOW TO DO THINGS WITH TEARS 1

How to do things with tears   3
Enough rain for Agnes Walquist   5
Elsie Young, aged pensioner, on Purgatory Mountain   10
Truluv the sailor   12
Brighter than glass   25
Epistola   26

Part Two WHITE SAILS   27

White sails: Notes toward the autobiography of an American poet 28
Dedicated to Irene on the threshold of the world   29
1. Hello!   31
2. LUTH. SCH.   32
3. The Chinese pot   34
4. White sales   35
5. The kiss-stone of the Fate   37
6. Winter road to the Cities   38
7. John the leaping deer   40
8. Cure   41
9. Marriage   43
10. Wallace Stevens entertains a sex worker   45

11. In the incomprehensible house   47

12. Stain   49

13. Her torn afghan   50

14. A woman and a girl feed pigs at sundown   53

15. A great jolt to start   55

16. Think again   56

*

Not all wanderers are lost   57

Part Three DO NOT BE CONTENT WITH AN
                    IMAGINARY GOD   63

Weird River   65

Flora's ABC: 6 Perseid sonnets, meteors of late August   66

SHAZAM!   69

Reason for eating pig   78

Latch: bespoke coffin-maker in purgatory   79

A Grand Caprice   81

Thunderstruck   84

X-rated   86

Your laughing lover   87

Crow   89

Star Asper   90

Part Four THREE NOTES ON COMMON CONCERNS
                    UNDER STAR ASPER   91

Note 1. Stanzas on pots   93

Note 2. Stanzas on poetic realism   94

Note 3. Ilona's letter   98

This is a HOW TO book. HOW TO DO THINGS WITH TEARS. The heroic singer of tradition is blind. The NEW singer in this present must be sighted. In this book the poet intends to say *something*, insofar as a poet can, about the common sadness of living and dying in the world.

At the center of the book is an autobiography of the SIGHTED SINGER, the American poet who has dreamed the dream of the poet's vocation—the demand that THIS person make sense of THIS world. In Part 4 of the book, THE POET says, in sentences, how such a thing can be done by poetic means and what the rules and logic of making sense *this* way might be.

The maxim of poetic thinking is: DO NOT BE CONTENT WITH AN IMAGINARY GOD. Poetry is the most realistic of arts. Poetic knowledge is useful KNOWLEDGE (knowledge that helps out with tears), but only when it encounters, and forces, into visibility (puts where you can see), whatever it is that resists your will to know and to love.

> *Ô saisons, ô châteaux!*
> *Quelle âmes est sans défauts?*
> Rimbaud

What these poems undertake to do

To make happen

thinking of a poetic kind
about common concerns.

If there are no common concerns
no experience the same for you and me

there can be no thinking of a poetic kind—maybe
no thinking at all.

Indeed, if it were possible to FIND by *this means*—
i.e., thinking of a poetic kind
COMMON CONCERNS

THAT WOULD AFTER ALL BE ENOUGH.

One great common concern is love which turns out
to be a story about finding

a hazardous pathway, mountain road, or river walk
hand in hand,

from the accident, thrownness, natality which was our
wandering into the world alone (somewhere—
ENIGMA, MN?)

to a general state of affairs (significance) which has
a kiss in it (holiness).

To find a pathway from natal accident (here? now?
why? no reason)

all the way to our mortal destination, the holy
state of these things

poems are the means I use.

PART ONE

HOW TO DO THINGS
WITH TEARS

How to do things with tears

In thy springs, O Zion, are the water wheels
of my mind! The wheels beat the shining stream.
Whack. Dying. And then death. *Whack.* Learning. Learned.
Whack. Breathing. And breath. *Whack.* Gone with the wind.

I am old. The direction of time is plain:
as the daylight, never without direction,
rises in a direction, east to west,
and sets in a direction, west to east,

walking backward all night long, underground;
so, this bright water is bent on its purpose—
to find the meadow path to the shore and then
the star ("Sleepless") by which the helmsman winds

and turns. Zion of the mind! This is the way:
toward nightfall the wind shifts offshore, north by
northwest, closing the harbor to sail,
and it stiffens, raising the metal water

in the roads. The low sun darkens and freezes.
The water shines. In the raking light is
towed the great ship home, upwind, everything
furled. And, behind the great ship, I am carried,

a castaway, in the body alone,
under the gates of Erebus—the meeting
place of daylight under ground and night wind
shrieking in wires, the halliards knocking and

raveled banners streaming to the southeast
like thought drawn out, wracked and torn, when the wind
shifts and rises and the light fails in the long
schoolroom of the setting sun. What is left

to mind but remembrances of the world?
The people of the road, in tears, sit down
at the roadside and tell stories of the world.
Then they rise in tears and go up.

The mill sits in the springs. The water wheel whacks
round: Alive. *Whack.* Dying. *Whack.* Dead. *Whack.* Nothing.
How then to do things with tears? —Deliver us,
Zion, from mist. Kill us in the light.

Enough rain for Agnes Walquist

(five little fits of tears)

We are all given something precious that we lose irrevocably.
                                                          Caproni

1.

It happened at midnight.
—What I possessed and lost
or what I never possessed
and have nonetheless lost,
or what in any case I
was not born possessing
but received from another's mouth:
—a smooth stone
passed in a kiss from the mouth
of a Fate into my open mouth
amidst odors of metal
and slamming doors
at the dark end of a railway car
as the train was leaning
on a curve and slowing
to stop—is lost. Lost
in that dark! —*Dilectissima,*
the Fate showed me two ways,
male and female. Also a third:
Gessert's midnight path
to the wild *iris,*
an escaped garden among
thickets of poison oak
where rolls the stony Oregon
and hears no sound
except stone on stone.

2.

What, then, shall I give YOU?
My kiss-stone is lost.
But look! The vast world,
energetic and empty,
glows in the dark.
On the strip between the road
—gravel or macadam,
or an earthen path
(but in this case gravel)
and the settlement
or the side-hill field or forest
or other tangled right of way
for jews, gypsies, ghosts
(outcasts in any case)
there among weeds
springs up Gessert's
wild *iris tenax*, violet or pale yellow,
the bloom 3" to 5" across.
Gessert asks, "How in the world
did they come here?"
Then he says, "If you must
take these *iris*,
use a shovel. Root them
in your garden
and let them go to seed.
Gather the seed
in Fall
—October or November.
Drive out into the countryside.
Plant the seeds
on any half-sunny,
slightly eroded, roadside bank.

Sow Gessert's *iris, dilectissima,*
Violet or ghostly yellow,
in the wild, universal garden
named "Shadowy Agnes Walquist,"
her midnight body
from which wild *iris*
and lilies grow.
To whom better entrust
pure loss?
To what breasts other
than the breasts
of Agnes Walquist!
—"Agnes! (Can you hear?)
when a man dies,
or a woman dies,
the whole world of which
he is the only subject
dies without residue
(or the whole world of which
she is the only subject
dies without residue).
'DID I EVER LIVE?'
NEVER, NEVER.'
The world of each person,
man or woman,
is a dependency of the world
of another one.
When a man dies or a woman
the reason for confidence
with respect to any world
is diminished. (Weep! Weep!)
When the last person but one
dies, the last person,
though he continue to live,
ceases to exist!"
Agnes Walquist sighs.
Then she says,
YES!

4.

In my sleep I say, "Agnes! I will
give you rain
from my mystery store
of rain. The dead have buried
the dead and are forever
burying the dead.
But the dead do not remember
as the living do not know
the heart." I wake
in the hour before dawn
to the huge hammer of the rain
(hammer of sex
as the poet makes it)
which thunders enough, enough, enough."
Earth shudders and springs.
The East grows bright.
And Agnes Walquist whispers,
"Thank you."

Sweet youth, sweet youth
(*dilectissima mea*)
go!
Punish thy pillow.
Your kiss-stone is among the stones
the stony Oregon rolls
and hears no sound
but stone on stone.
Blond Fate, the honey-blond,
no longer knows which one
is the stone of witness.
What follows is the wearing
out to dust.
The water mill deep down
in ocean grinds out salt
(truth, troth, death).
But sweeter than the body
of a man or a woman
(sweetness of that sweetness,
song of all those songs)
is the midnight garden
of Agnes Walquist.
Her breasts are sweet.
The huge hammer is an ancient memory
of water falling into water.
There is lightening all night
on distant mountains,
strike after strike
(violet, blue, red, ghostly yellow,
indigo).
And along the mountain paths,
asleep or dead,
are sprawled
nocturnal mountaineers.

Elsie Young, aged pensioner, on Purgatory Mountain

1.

Then we came upon a woman with a black cat
on her knees. Among its many noticeable defects
one was that it was dead. Of what did the cat die?
The cat died of *desire* which is a relentless dis-
position to solve hard problems—as one might say,
to get to the other side of the road despite the
trucks. The woman says, *"Let there be nothing left out."*
"But if nothing is to be left out," replies the dead cat,
"nevertheless one must not cross the road in traffic."
He has learned from his experience. As for the woman,
at the inquest traces of no fatal mistake
will be detected anywhere on her body. *Dilectissima,*
our business is to wander up the footpath
hand in hand, telling one another what there
is to see on Purgatory Mountain. "There's
the gate," we say. "On it everything possible

2.

to be arrived at, and seen, by passing through any gate
is inscribed. This gate is called MORNING LIGHT.
We must agree, you and I, not to be kind to ones
who darken the way with secrecy. But to those others
who say our name and tell a good story we turn
and say in reply, 'It is well to start early, in the hour
before dawn and in the silence of seeing nothing
while things are still wrapped in their nature and night,
the limit of our eloquence, is toward the end of its patrol.'"
—The first person we met on the mountain, after the material
sun (the sun itself, not its reflection in the mind) appeared
above the horizon like the soul of water rising in the eye
of one who has thought upon water a long time, was Elsie
Young, pensioner—eyes like bright water. She arose,
brushing the dead cat from her lap, which had replied
as I have told you, about "desire", etc.—a long gab,
but now it is finished. Elsie holds a glass of water up,
the work of a lifetime, to the morning light. She says,
triumphant: "I am as a sparrow alone on a housetop."

3

The wind rose and Elsie Young vanished with a cry
like a leaf blown upward. —*"Tell me, kid.* Among all lives
which is the *admirable* life?" Owen Barfield asked *me*
that question long ago—a Steinerian, an anthroposo-
phist, one who KNEW. (He is dead, I presume. Shall we
see him, then, on this mountain in his rough shoes,
good for walking the uneven earth?) Owen Barfield loved
and married Alice, a woman much older than himself.
He saw what others cannot see: the inmost sentiments
of certain persons, which appeared to him like colored
scarves, or gaudy snoods or veils—fountainous red
for utter thought and, for desire, watery blue. Listen,
up here the sound of many waters speaks as a god
speaks out of his synclinal fold, feeding
willows, leathery amaranth, insatiable bamboo—and also
(their stainless 18-wheelers idling on the beach below)

4.

among these cooling rocks the slaughtering gangs. . . .
—Beyond the gate called MORNING LIGHT, beyond gate ZENITH,
and gate AFTERNOON there looms, mysterious and austere,
gate CREPUSCULE, high up, crowned with a gibbous moon.
See how, among dark waters, soaked through by streams,
they sit, done with the Great Work now, all four: stylish
Owen Barfield, sporting the cerulean voiles of his desire;
blushing Alice, always in her wedding gown; and Elsie,
aged pensioner, whose income's (as you know) secure.
On her lap the dead cat, overdressed as usual, in fur,
having thrown caution to the winds, stares back in rapture
over its left shoulder, starry eyed, at Elsie Young, heroine
of the admirable life,and whispers *sotto voce* (under its breath),
"'Take pleasure as your guide.' But remember, feed the pet!
And always, dead or alive, my sparrow, carry a knife."

Truluv the sailor

le dernier couac de Rabbi Tarfon

There is some way the world is and also
some way the inner world, fierce female visitor
by night, is, who beats the ground and cries out
"aicha," "aicha." I myself have heard her,
and still do hear her, cry the names of her god.
—Where your treasure is, there is your heart also.
O my particular student, where is your heart?

You can see for yourself, kid! —That's the ruin
on the precipice at Deep—a wild resort.
Far below the ruin, using my Zeiss
field glasses, I made sketches: *remembrances*
of the world. Then as we approach, successive
apertures reveal buttresses. And a row
of beautifully shaped, arched window-openings
in Gothic style came into view. It seemed
a cathedral and full of magic. But when
quite near, I saw that in sober reality
the walls were barely 24 feet high
and also, inexorably, the sea
had devoured the cliff, sea-sounds made inaudible
the sermon, the whole church doomed to wrack and ruin.

—"An ocean of voices has stormed ashore
at Deep since the beginning of the world.
Each voice speaks out loud when the wind is up.
Each voice is singular, lost in thought,
though water. And the intricate black breakers
are tenements of many rooms. In each room
is one chair and in each chair sits a man
or woman thinking: 'What *was not*,' they think
'comes to be.' And what comes to be infallibly
passes into memory. And what passes into
memory may become, for a time, a song.
Then it vanishes. Songs vanish, they do
not end. It is infinity, the dying
without the death, ruins the house of God.

"O kid, standing at this shore, the earth
exploding about us as the storm waves
strike the rock, I wonder there *can* be traffic
between shores so distant and so disturbed!
But to the river mouth the daily boats come home.
—No longer twilight, it is now night.
A huge sun has gone down into the ocean.
All roads and other public ways on earth
are dark. And ocean with the air above it
(also a public way) is dark and void
as it was in the beginning. The paths
are deserted of their children and forest
tracks unknown—not yet remembered, or never
again remembered—by men or by animals.

"'When comes the long awaited, the orient pearl?'
—What the beginning meant is discovered
to mind only at the end of the story
(or more precisely near the end of the story
for the end is nothing.) Then, great desire
wells up in you (in me, O kid!) like water,
the only *great* desire there is: to know
the outcome as we approach the source.
Look there! A boat of some kind (notice how
it scorns all human instruments, and seeks
no oar, nor engine, nor other sail than wings)
heaves to upwind and sends ashore a naked man,
the blue jewel of the whole story in his eye
(the lights, the signals, and the colors of it).

"And YOU are the woman who sees him
because of the blue jewel in the sailor's eye.
His penis grows thick and all that goes with *that*.
Think of it, kid, huge and heavy in your hand!
Sex flows from life to death. Between the arousal
of the pilgrim who takes the blue-eyed sailor
in her arms and the consummation of her passion
(and the long sleep) extends this too brief vigil
of the senses—ascent with others on the mountain
as the song of the blue-eyed sailor, from
the beach, grows faint and fainter and the rains
come. —Night on the mountain is full of thunder
in the hour before dawn, the darkest one.
At last, the sun's light brightens the uplands.

"O lambs! Follow us to school on the mountain.
Something is coming to pass on the blue floor
of the schoolroom in the rising light.
Some children go to school alone on the heights.
Others go, smiling, in company of friends
and animals.—Today, there are three of us
at the start: myself (the one with the Zeiss), YOU
kid, whoever you are, and a dog named Butch,
a famous hound whose real name is unknown.
(People—as you may have noticed—don't say much.
But if you have a dog with you more gets said.
Look a dog intently in the eye, any dog!
It may recite an astounding poem to you.)
Higher still, upon the summit out of sight

"where are perpetual snows and icy springs
and fiery altars daily ignited,
and the ceaseless bells, the mountain sheep
unshorn go to water. How like a school-
house in a field of flax this mountain stands
in the blue acre of ocean—on which the wind
(darkening the voices) has been at work night
and day since the beginning of the world.
(And God knows what yet may come from the water!)
But now, on the floor of the schoolhouse, something
is coming to pass at last in the blue light.
NOW as at the hour of our death a man
or a woman stares at his own body, or
at her own body. He sees the irreparable

"wound of which he must die. 'It cannot heal,'
he says. She, too, sees the irreparable wound
which cannot heal. 'It cannot heal,' she says.
The god supplies the mountain and the path.
The poet supplies these chains. And the winds,
which are the strange sounds of her pleasure,
wander the steep slopes of the island mountain
(my Jew purgatory) both night and day.
—At first, seen from far off, in the low light
of a huge sun going down beneath the great
acre of ocean—at the punctual moment
of the disappearance of the track, now
filling up with new snow—on the left hand,
behind the rock buttresses of the mountain

"and in the serene air of evening (darkening
yet crystalline)—*there suddenly appeared*
an energetic insect of great size or,
maybe, a naked animal covering its excrement.
But then, as we approached, we saw it was,
in fact, a desolate woman. She scratched
the stone, working with the nails of both hands
at a dark patch on the snow as if she
had spilled black ink on rock. However violently
she scratched the stain was there for all to see,
'What god,' I thought, 'or demon has decreed
this labor (as it were) of burying a story
and d*igging up the same story—forever*.'
'Aicha,' 'aicha,' she cries and beats the ground.

"As I stood behind her, looking down at
her spread buttocks into which her heels pressed.
The mountain shook. She fell flat as if violated.
Then rose, turned around covering her shame,
and spoke to me—: 'OK! I am just now dead
so I can't say yet how things will come out
now I have left behind the burning farm,
the freezing wash, the screaming animals
"No longer in Lethean foliage caught."
Then she said, 'Pigs are cleaner than some people.
City people, for example (with "indoor
plumbing"), shit in their own houses. But pigs
shit outside, as country men and women do—
and then wander on under the wintry stars,

"'Across the stubble of the home field, all
the way to the Ice Palace on the frozen lake:—
a clean cold bedroom and cold bed, with walls
and stainless sheet and coverlet of ice.'
Then she said, 'I am Irene. —Don't look at me.
Don't touch me. Do *not* say my name. Every flake
of snow that fell in the garden, Oct. 23
1939, every infant fallen from the sky,
is on this mountain still. What are these snows?
The return of souls, silent and composed.'
—'Then *where are* the snows of yesteryear?
Where *are* they?' I ask. —'Well, look around you.
They're right over there.' —'Where?' —'Over *there*
in the shade of the rock where the sun never

" 'comes.' —'And where is Eloise whom I adore?'
—'She's over there, too, sitting in the snow
lecturing the animals.' And it was so:
'*Amo ergo sum,*' I heard her say. 'There is
EVENING KNOWLEDGE and MORNING KNOWLEDGE, every day.'
As Eloise spoke, the sunken path darkened
and the cold snake edged in toward the white dust
at the center of the path which was still warm.
Eloise, sitting in the melting snow,
turned from her animals and addressed the mountain,
'To my master who is also a father,
to my husband who is also a brother,
his handmaid who is also his sister and
wife and daughter and mother, Heloise!

" 'Bruno, Bruno of the many worlds! Does
the moon move, a "ghostly galleon tossed upon
cloudy seas"? Is the road "a ribbon of silver"?
Or do the clouds move and the moon stand still
in an infinite pool? Kiss, kiss, Master Bruno.
I beg you. Your Eloise wants to know!
No more stories. Think what you owe me, my true-
love. Give us rules.' —Then, the blue-eyed sailor's song
(called 'EVENING KNOWLEDGE') rises from the beach
and reaches to the highest tower of the darkening
mountain, among eagles and their thoughts:
'How salutary to go to the sick or the dead.
It is better to visit a house of mourning,
my beloved, than a house of feasting

"'for to be mourned is the lot of everyone.
The body of the dead woman must be washed
at once by the sisters, clad in some cheap
but clean garment and stockings and laid
on a bier, the head covered by a veil.
These coverings must be firmly stitched or bound
to the body and not afterwards removed.
The body shall be carried into the church.
Meanwhile, the sisters shall devote themselves
to psalm-singing and prayer in the oratory.
The burial of an abbess shall have one feature
to distinguish it from that of others:
her entire body shall be wrapped in a hair
shirt and sewn up in it as in a sack.'

"The sailor's song stopped. Night descended from its tower.
We slept, and the world was without us for a time.
—I know sleep of two kinds: the *first* sleep is
waiting for what may come, a sort of patience,
but wearisome and a continual disgrace,
seeing nothing but the dark and hearing nothing
but the street. The *second* sleep is without end:
suddenly at the shore with others where,
from the river mouth, the daily boats depart
east by northeast into the eye of the storm.
Thus do sail the unborn and the lovers, dead upwind.
The skies send down bolt after shining bolt
into the earth of the far shore. And we lean
on the rail together staring at the dark

"and the falling fire which we take to heart.
Look, kid! Between the world and the poem of
the world, there is the difference of great sanity.
The poem of the world is great sanity
but the world is another thing—or nothing.
If there is to be a poet, then there must
be great sanity. 'For sure,' they will say.
'In that person there is sometimes great sanity,
more than in trees.' For, when there's a poem,
another may walk out with the page in hand,
at evening, and may read it by the light
that is still left. And the neighbors become
apparitional and the horned cows that mourn
among the sallows where the path runs through
the meadow—at the low dark place—and disappears.

—"When we awakened, it was Good Shepherd Sunday.
We sat up and listened in the morning dusk
to the quick water-stream—*lymphae loquaces*—
bright talk in the dark—falling from the melt
of spring snows above: 'O tribute of wild tears!'
How many of us?—Irene (retired peasant);
Eloise (wet trousers) at her prayers and
letter writing; Me (the Jew); Bruno, well-
hung blue-eyed sailor (he had come up somehow
in the night), old as the world; one kid (YOU);
and the talking dog formerly called Butch.
The ocean was still dark and the sky overcast
except for certain light-driven clouds eastward,
far out near the horizon beneath which the dawn

"shown on the water like a clearing in a wood.
The light was rising on Zion and its springs
which is to say: 'On the mountain we met.'
—*Ocean screamed.* But the sailor was patient. He
had had enough. And, then, out of the darkness,
from around a bend of the path, MORNING KNOWLEDGE
itself came into view—top of the line—
with lights flashing like a Christmas tree,
hatchback up and, on the tape deck: 'Never cross
the sweet-flowing waters of ever-rolling
rivers placing the left foot *before* the right.'
In the car was a tall dark women, naked
and looking good. The dog-poet, 'Butch,' moaned.
And Edith Stein, Carmelite, placing her *right*
foot before her left, stepped down from her limousine.

"'I am Sancta Edith. I was once a Jew.
Now I am a Christian. This mountain is
my desert. Abbess Eloise is my friend.
I was killed naked so I now *am* naked.
Look at me.' Butch licked her toe but said nothing.
'It had always seemed to me that our Lord
was keeping something for me in the mountain
that could only be found *there.* And it opened
at last on 21 April 1938, in Easter Week.
In deep peace I stepped across the threshold
into the house of the Lord. That was why
the mountain shook and Irene fell down hard.
I am naked now. But I will get a new dress
where the flax is threshed in sapphire light,

"'and the strands spun, then woven, the cloth cut
and the garment sewn on the schoolhouse floor.
I say this to all of you, but particularly
to the old guy with the Zeiss field glasses
and sketch pad (remembrancer of the world)
and to the bedroom-blue-eyed sailor, well-
hung troubadour of one drone, a song of first knowledge
("How can I miss you, if you won't go away," etc.):
in *my* Purgatory all stories are
suspended, for a time, in the blue light
of outcome. Then, they disappear. All life
disappears. It does not end indifferent
to outcome—it disappears. Every poem,
rightly conducted, i.e., without looking away

"'from the wound, is a test: *whether* the maker
of the poem can endure the *one* coherent
conclusion to which the poem has led him.
Whether he is willing to know what is
given him to know and willing to be seen
as one who knows precisely that. Or whether she
is willing to know what she is given to
know and to be seen knowing precisely that.
In any case, such is first knowledge, the
bottom of the hole. Jew! Have you forgotten?
You will die waiting in the same way that
the rock is devoured by ocean, so that
all the sacred places fall and disappear
in water—and the grove lacks an altar.

" 'Most of the life of men and women is spent
waiting and so the greater part of a man
or woman dies waiting, body and soul,
dies and what he is waiting for *is* death
and what she is waiting for is death also.
The body and consciousness of the body
are waiting but the ocean does not wait.
Neither patient nor impatient the sound
of the wave and the blue light. . . . ' " —Suddenly,
on the cliff side of the path a gouged-up root
with a voice like Shelley screamed, "Sancta Edith,
meine Schwester, what does Aquinas say?
Straw, STRAW? I am Rabbi Tarfon. Some of
US eat straw." He also said, "Death can overtake

"a man only when he is idle, for
it is written God WILL not overshadow
Is-ra-el until her work is done.
But now she cries, fierce female visitor
in Zion, bearded sibyl by night beating the
ground: '*Aicha! There is some way the world is.*'
O kid! From the highest rock of my Jew
purgatory, when the eye-beam which all
this time has wandered abroad, at last
inherits its beautiful estate, then
unless the poet falsify his report
you can see all the way to the next room.
Over that window evening is drawing in
and slowly the curtain of night drawn down."

Truluv, the sailor, and the Abbess Eloise
reread their story, this time through to the end,
because it is now written through to the end.
They sit together and think about it.
The waves come ashore at Deep. The beach shudders,
smooths itself, and is still. All the watery rooms
are empty of their shadows. Eloise changes
out of her wet clothes and walks upward alone.
Truluv, the blue-eyed sailor, goes back to work,
first mate on the Ghostly Galleon that carries
Edith Stein as supercargo. Irene is dramaturge
because she knows how things come out in the end.
This poem is the dernier couac *of Rabbi Tarfon.*
Hereafter, the cobalt text—oblivion.

Brighter than glass

Never yet having gone all the way over to the well of tears
in the interest of thinking of the poetic kind, I am
like the face—white, leaflike—of a man whose tears
cannot be seen, plastered on the window of a railway car at
the punctual instant of passing, as at the yelling birth of
a mortal soul (the immortals are born very quietly)

when the Fates in their "stiff, painted clothes," blind mostly
(you will remember the honey-blond), and with smooth unrealized
countenances (as yet they might be anything with a face)
foregather having wandered in, strangers to one another,
to a place uncertain at the appointed time. Take note, beloved!
The world is empty but the heart is full. Birdsong follows

the trains across great plains of dream all the way over
to the well of tears. Toward that certain place leads on
the railroad ribbon of silver. Rise heart! You have slumbered
a whole life and dreamed the dream of the divided throat
and begotten children (five straight arrows against the enemy).
Rise, heart, with me from this bed of loves no longer young,

like a soul whose name is well known. As when death is at hand
the Fates of the birth-instant return better acquainted and
with faces not imaginary. Drink deep (they say) or drink not
of the well of tears. *Splendidior vitro.* It glows in a dark
place where the leaves (the oak, the beech) lie whitening
each over each from the beginning of the world.

The God fell silent forever on the day he saw earth.
He said to her ONCE: "You. I want you to be." O kid!
The God we serve requires nothing of us. Not even death.

Epistola

"O kid! I sit on a chair in the dark.
Outside the window dawn has not come up.

The cat cries like a widow at a grave.
Just now I am the only Jew in the world.

God says to himself, 'What shall I do NOW?'
And then he says to me, 'Grossman, you are

the only Jew that is. It's up to you.'
So I ask him, 'What happened to the rest

of the Jews. Then God says, 'Put out the cat.'
—O kid! What shall I do? It is still dark

but the sky lightens over the machinery.
It's up to us. ONE is not enough.

Look! Dawn is coming up the harbor. A-
drift in the roads is a masterless schooner

and in the rigging of it the four-legged
widow fast asleep. O kid! if you ever

get this *epistola* come and see me. May-
be we can make a Jew out of you yet."

PART TWO

WHITE SAILS

White sails:

Notes toward the autobiography of an American poet

> *Das Herz ist satt. Die Welt ist leer.*
> The heart is full. The world is empty.
> Novalis

Dedicated to Irene at the threshold of the world

Odors of peonies hold you, *dilectissima,*
echoing odors of announcement. "What ho!"

At the moment when mind becomes *intelligible*
to itself, it immediately reaches a limit.

The city falls down and meadowland blackens.
Dilectissima, your beautiful hair!

At the moment when mind becomes intelligible
to itself, the poem of the mind intelligible

to itself is heard echoing in the distance,
like odors of the garden *we* know of.

The road traverses blackened meadows, rises,
and disappears. —I cannot comfort you.

Mother of every virgin, you are come
to term this time at the limit. What now?

What song? What words of a song? —At the limit,
when the mind becomes intelligible

to itself, the first birth cry ever heard
is heard, because the poem of the sufficiency

of the mind has stopped. There is no sound.
But the cry, always going on, *can now*

be heard because there is no other song,
no echoing in the distance where the city

once stood and flourished. Only the poets' shout,
the poem of the mind at the limit of mind:

the *erub,* sacred thread, the edge beyond
which you cannot carry anything on the Sabbath,

not even a child. But do not be afraid.
Your hair is beautiful. The destination

of your breasts is toward the sea. Be assured
nothing will suffice. The mind has crossed over

and *stopped cold* at the threshold of the world.

1.

Hello!

iam redidet virgo
now returns the girl
Eclogue 4

In the Land of Lakes the sky says blue, blue,
not minding to repeat itself. In fact, happy.

Or the sky whispers rain, rain. Or dark, dark,
dark. Or snow.

White sails on the lake peck, peck at the sky
until, suddenly, a great Augur Hawk labors up

(I hear it now. I'm looking another way.
Then I turn around and see it with two eyes.)

out of the high grass behind my back,
a serpent in its claw, hawk and serpent

near at hand, on this side of the fence.
The sky hails *me*: "YOU. KID. VICTORIOUS!

—Where the water darkens, the winds succeed.
This is the law of white sails: YOU SHALL SUCCEED.

The north wind HAZARD, the west wind SPEED,
the south wind SEX, the east TREACHERY.

Now the blue blue *virgo* returns.
A born child smiles and says, "HELLO!"

2.

Luth. Sch.

On the 7th of January, 1931,
Irene Victorious Stadtherr

whose mother was
Victorious Beret

(who, though dead and in the grave,
appears to her in time of need)

left Gibbon, Minnesota.
I am a poet, Irene said.

I will do penance
for the whole world.

This is my ETERNAL work.
Irene planned it out.

I will take a Greyhound
bus (carefully putting my

pot from China
under the seat of the driver)

to the Cities to look
for work. I'm not crazy

about housework. But
nothing else is offering.

Mother Victorious whispers,
"Today we are going

to the Cities.
Follow me."

Irene followed past LUTH. SCH.
and the haunted house

at the crossroads.
The town was thin, fragile,

like a worn sheet.

The Chinese pot*

Mind is a pot.
Let it stand forever
against the leakiness

of things. If crazed
("crazed" means broken.),
the stain is *black*.

The body is a pot.
May it not leak,
our beautiful body.

The face,
primordial first text,
is the honorable ornament

of the skull pot.
Weeping it says, "Sing
me something."

For song is also a pot,
a fence, and a seal
unbreakable, unless

the mind pot
be cracked.
A lamp

is a pot.
When it shatters,
the light, as the poet

Shelley said,
in dust
lies dead.

*See note "Note 1. Stanzas on pots," p. 93 below.

4.

White sales

The bus stops uptown
next to the John Deere.

The step from the paving
into the bus is high.

How did Irene get on the bus?
This is a trouble.

"I am not a tall girl."
She thought she would take the

train on the way back:
"But I, even as the dogs,

feel a yearning
for the infinite. . . . I cannot,

I *cannot* satisfy that hunger!
I am the daughter of a man and a woman.

I had thought to be more than this.
If it had been left to me. I would much

rather have been the daughter of
a shark."

*

On the bus Irene talked to a fat
blind woman. They talked about

January White Sales. The blind
woman was going to the Cities

to buy sheets. She said
"Percale," "Lotus Bloom,"

"Egyptian Cotton."
Then the fat, blind, honey-

blond Fate kissed Irene.
From the mouth of the

Fate a stone passed
into the mouth of the girl

who then said *"I have begun.
I go up from where I was thrown*

to where *I shall betake myself.*
There Solomon in all his glory

shall receive his queen."

The kiss-stone of the Fate

"Now you shall remember what I remember:
At midnight the still air fills with fragrance,
many desires become, at last, melodiously one desire.
I awoke, burdened by the gravity of the fragrance
—a soul waking at midnight
astonished to find herself as one who is
upon the pathway of the moth-god that visits
CEREUS, the *night-blooming*. The moth-god said,
'Sing me something.' I sang, for the first time,
as a flower sings that blooms only once and only
at midnight and only for the one who loves her.
Then the god kissed me and a stone passed
from the mouth of the god into my open mouth.
Now it is your stone.

> *Dilectissima*, song is divine
thought. The nature of 'divine thought' is
complex. Although THOUGHT is held to be the most
divine of phenomena, the question what it must be
in order to have that character involves difficulties.
Go to the Cities. Find the poet S—— who is old as
the world. (Someone must be as old as the world.)
He knows or does not know."

Finally, the honey-blond said: "This is how to do
things with tears:—remember what I remember.
Do not remember me."

Winter road to the Cities

"We are close to waking when we dream
about dreaming"

said Charles Flandrau, hero of the siege
of New Ulm, remembering what he remembered.

"The Sioux were at the door. The winter
road was strewn with once loved objects.

The store-keepers opened their stores and
offered their wares without compensation.

The love of possessions which forms the
mainspring of life disappeared in this

forced retreat: things were abandoned and
lost, not once but many times.

A half-opened package of knives.
Mark the place it can be found again.

Mark it, mark it. But there is no mark
in this storm, among these snows.

My wife had received a glass sugar bowl
from one of the merchants. As she and the children

were mounting the wagon, the driver
declared that she was forbidden

to burden the wagon with such objects.
My wife declared it was pity to destroy

them and then offered to give them to him.
He quickly accepted them placing them under

the seat, their weight forgotten,
and whipped up the horses.

Blown snow made indistinguishable
the home-field, and the winter road

to the stone-carved city, rose-red."

John the leaping deer

Irene's father worked at the John Deere
selling tractors, harrows, seed drills,
manure spreaders, combines, etc.
But there was not much traffic lately.
On the green enameled metal of each machine
is a leaping deer. The Deere is an upward,
animal, always in midleap. The metal is clean,
odorless, without flaw, reflecting light
with a face in it (her own)
and it is cold, condensing breath (her own).
Her father's name is John, like the Deere.
Now he is dying in a room off the kitchen
close to the iron stove, an abandoned wagon
rotting in a cold wet pasture. Despite
the stove, John's room is always filled
with abandonment, cold and wet.
Irene says out loud, "What thou lovest best
DOES NOT REMAIN VERY LONG."
(Victorious is of the same opinion.)
Jesus of the Bleeding Heart hangs on the wall
behind John's head. John cannot see him.
Jesus' heart is bleeding. He feels John's
pain and knows John will die. Jesus repeats
to himself, "What thou lovest best lingers
but does not remain very long." Jesus, too,
is troubled because the poet was wrong.
John is patient but has never seen or
been seen, by anyone. Irene thinks,
"Another poem is needed. THAT'S WORK."
(Victorious is of the same opinion.)

Cure

"JE SUIS L'IMMACULÉE CONCEPTION" (Lourdes)
"ICH BIN DIE UNBEFLECKTE EMPFÄNGNIS" (New Ulm)

On the lakes, white sails! Strength of many
wings. Such wings carried Our Lady of Lourdes
from France, as by angels. Great wind-wings
of thought, in fact circling the world, made
a grotto and a crossroad where were no roads,
no marks before that, on the great plain of dream.
This beautiful body (*dilectissima*) can only
come from a beautiful *body*, born not made.
What else is strong enough to do the WORK
of the human world, body of our life and face
of our greeting. (Victorious smiled knowingly
but said nothing out loud, thinking, "divine"
means strong enough to make sense, "immaculate"
means clear enough to make useful sense.)

On that occasion what did the virgin wear?
What was suitable for travel by white sails?
Her shoes were of particular concern. How happy
Irene (also a smart traveler) is to see Her shoes:
charming (Gimbel's exclusive) silk slippers, embroidered
with tiny wild field flowers. The rest of the outfit,
entirely handmade silk lingerie, and (underneath?)
Alençon lace close to the body. To Bernadette alone
(for sure) and not to other girls, until Irene,
did she, dressed as she should be dressed, appear.

The intelligence of white sails is this: *from a great distance comes the wind*, never a casual fact, but result of intricate histories, like a glance on which everything depends, the yes and no of power. The path it takes over the hills to the lake is known to few. But at the shore it is seen by all, a darkening. *From a great distance also comes the sail*, cut, sewn, rigged, set, by other answering hands, and now manned and headed by one hand which turns towards the wind with care *never to stare*. The eye of the wind, immaculate, stops thought. By seeking and averting, finding and then losing, the will learns the cure. But, coming to moor, you must know the direction of the wind and turn into it. As you approach the end do not be distracted by the book, that strange control to which the mind is irresistibly drawn. In all that fury, swear by the moon.

9

Marriage

Feast of the Circumcision

Following Bernard's prescription
she cast off her tunic (in Oyster Bay,
where all grand marriages occur).
On the tennis courts there
Solomon in all his glory
receives his queen.
"A Jew at last!"
cries Irene.
"And circumcised,
as the Fate said he would be,
on the eighth day
like John." (Luke 1:59)

Then she thought, I will bear his child
(Victorious did not approve),
and his child will *know*.
His wife is named Beatrice.
I must meet her. All poets do
meet Beatrice.
"She will make me cry,"
Irene says.
"But it is not my job to console the world."
(Victorious approved.)

Then Irene did what was required
and wisdom flowed.
"There will be a child."

But what is the new poet's name?
As can still be seen in the register,
the name was written and crossed out
and re-written in a futile effort to cancel
or change the name of the newborn.
(His namesake had absconded with funds.)
The effort was ineffectual.
The first name of the new poet
can be seen
through the erasure.

The wedding on the tennis court
is known from pictures. The bride wore
a princess gown and long court train
(as was proper in the case)
which fell from her waist
and was surmounted by a tulle veil
and a cap of rose-point lace.
Also, the bride carried a bouquet
of gardenias, lilies of the valley,
and white orchids—
dark myth left empty
at her death.

10

Wallace Stevens entertains a sex worker

A throw of the dice will not abolish hazard
                                    Mallarmé

Nicollette hotel
corner Nicollette and Hennepin
7th floor above the
Milwaukee road.
Gateway district.
Red light.

SHAZAM! There sits
wizard Stevens
(the poet S—)
claims adjuster
(not himself a party)
a planet on

his table.
He is devising
the abolition
of accident
by actuarial
means,

poetry.
Perfect insurance.
He will tell me
what I want to know.
He will show me what I
want to see.

What I want
to know is
what the God
thinks about
at the end of
the Milwaukee road.

Shazam says
about *seeing*
better not to see
some things
than to
see them.

Shazam says
about thinking
the God's thinking
is best thinking.
Thinking about
thinking.

That's fine
says Irene
he's thinking
about thinking,
my body.
Irene sirene.

11.

In the incomprehensible house

However intimate the room, however well known the bed,
the book, the sounds—morning, noon, and night,
the odors of other bodies, the noisy traffic of dying,
fucking, and being born—I am, nonetheless, always outside,
wandering among strangers and the house incomprehensible.

If you sleep long enough, you come to this house.
I have slept long enough. The dream of dreaming
is the last dream before waking—
the portentous story of waking never to dream again.
The afternoon has led us to the Ice Palace

on Nokomis. In despite of King Sun, a mirrorless
pile, with stairs, and rails, rooms and streaming walls
of rooms, tables, chairs, all ice, a metal without history
or expectation, the brilliant melting lake of each moment.
I saw you but I did not meet you in the dream

of the incomprehensible house. Here sun rises
and the palace melts, becomes fresh water, streams toward
Nokomis from which it flows out, night after night, into
the salt sea. The salt sea is the incomprehensible house.
All houses are mansions of ocean incomprehensible.

There was a house across First Street from the church.
First Street was the town crease, as of a bottom sheet
worn thin by use. Behind the house a path led,
first to an iron pump, and then to the chicken coop
and the slaughtering barrel. Behind the chickens was a

barn, with three cows and a chained dog. Behind the barn
was a cornfield. On Christmas morning everyone in the
incomprehensible house went to midnight Mass and the three
cows knelt where they stood and gave thanks to see, once
again, an infant asleep in hay the family left special.

But the chained dog howled incessantly from
that day his master, the eldest son (worked in the
creamery), went to the wars, and did not cease howling
Christmas or any other day, as if *there was a God*,
whose only prophet was this desolate animal.

12.

Stain

Irene awakened and arose to tell her dream
of the all-mirroring incomprehensible house.
She sat down to write with her left hand,
her writing hand, a letter to her father John,
a left-handed man. But her right hand, the un-
writing hand, threw down the ink bottle (how
could that be!), shattered it, and so spilled black
ink on a beautiful rug (not her own, of course)
making *an ineradicable stain of the unwritten.*
Everything possible to be written,
now unwritten forever. She worked and worked
with all her strength, until the beautiful rug
was worn, threadbare, erased, no longer beautiful.
But the unwritten letter—spilled ink of all lost
letters to the world—cannot be cleaned from
the rug. "House work is not for me. The unwritten
cannot become the written. The mind murdered
by men or by God is not. Father of consciousness
(the poet's prayer), I must leave this place,
this black pool of the unwritten, inerasable mark
of what cannot be repented. My errant
right hand has returned all other words to
the black lamp.
I am in a strange house, a house of many cries
where the waters run by Babylon
and leave no trace, no warrantable testimony
of what is past, passing, or yet to come.
I will follow the deer upward as it dies."

13.

Her torn afghan

(Irene at Christmas Lake MN, Jan. 7 1932)

"Rest before labour"

1.

White sails on black seas. White white word
on damask snow written, "Rest before labour,

Thunderous lake." Damascene also the selvage.
Embroidered crowns, snow-white, adorn the shore,

the hemlock, the pine under snow, and the uttering oak:
"O black ice, A NEW THOUGHT. The sun's not at all.

Was never. This is the hour after or before,
echoless. But something is coming to pass.

Rest before labour. Sprawl." White white white white
Beatrice rests under her torn afghan.

Is THAT house work? "It's up to you, ladies. Spend.
The poor need employment, in a dark time."

2.

What was on offer? —I'm not crazy about house work,
poet American, sex worker, *now* house keeper.

Front stairs, masterful, winding into light.
Back stairs, straight up (or down) to the dark house.

This servant rested there and listened, in the second
house, a grave with a stained carpet, to the fucking—

house work in the next room over. Then a Dream
visited Irene and the Dream wrote on illiterate

blackboard, on the black hawk-augur sky, "YOU, sing me
something!" (Victorious says, "It doesn't mean *me*.")

And Irene does sing: "This is the hour before the dawn,
when the white sails are folded on the mast.

3.

"In the Cities, we do the sheets in hard
white water, from god knows where. In the country,

we do the sheets in soft brown rainy water.
It comes from the roof. Easy to see how:

On dark days the clouds let down water for washing
and the roof darkens it, soft water for washing

not drink: soap-making, washing, rinsing, blueing,
hanging-out, blowing in the wind (no stain without

remedy). Summer—or winter in the freezing air—
dark water washes white, no Rinso!

Then gentile and Jew fold away
laundry.

4.

"Men and women are happier if there is
a profound work, less tearful,

not so violent.
The black lake knows the sun approaches,

winds stir the air, search the creased furl.
NOW thunderous report. NOW echo thunderous.

The sun is coming to be—in style.
An ice boat tacks upwind

gathering the meaning of things,
white sails in the dark.

What you know is what there is to know,
for sure.

5.

"Mother Beatrice sleeps in the afternoon
under her torn afghan,

afghan for lying alone, afghan for repose,
rest before labour.

Profound
the worn bottom sheet unfurls birth thought,

sex thought, breath thought, death thought,
white sails.

When the singer is sighted the woman
or the man who sings, unblind,

sees in the sunrise, this time, a sun
which shall have no line."

14.

A woman and a girl feed pigs at sundown

"A people . . . that sacrificeth in gardens. . . . Which remain among the graves, and lodge in the monuments . . . and eat swine's flesh. . . ."

Isaiah 65: 3, 4.

Pigs do not remember Jerusalem. I hunger.
I have a hunger, as deep as the sea,
to forget Jerusalem. I commit my right
hand (all its famous cunning) to oblivion.
When they ask for a song I shall open
my throat and sing the song of the conscious
animal, garden and grave—*unbeflekte*.
We exist in order to say to one another:
"We are all captive animals of the
Babylonian death world. That makes us
careful and cleanly in our habits.
We are the source and we are the consumed.
The pig knows not Jerusalem. That is
wonderful.

On the wild mountains of X,
we celebrate the forgetting of Jerusalem
among pigs, where the right hand is always
without cunning and Jerusalem disappears
for whole nights which are very quiet.
Our song has never been heard before in
the world.

But in the half-dark evening,
after the cows are milked and the milk
separated and the separator

washed, a girl and her mother manhandle
the waste skim milk in an aluminum
can, as tall as the girl is, across a shadowy
barnyard to the pigs' trough. Then the girl, alone,
carries down the sodden swill of the day's
leavings in a white enamel pail from
the house to the pigs' stye and scatters the
offal among the swine. And the girl, alone,
cleans the white enamel pail in the horse
trough and fills it slowly with cold water
from the well. She says, 'It is as if a
cloudless sky were, first, below in the mirroring
white pail of clear water, and, then, above me
in the mineral blue evening weighted beyond
my strength with the whole darkness of night
over my head.'"

A great jolt to start

Back by train
Jan. 7, THURS., 1932. It was cold
in Minnesota.
Can you believe it? 20 below at midday!
On the train (in the third car of three, a caboose)
there was an iron stove on which was written
IF I AM GOOD TELL OTHERS ABOUT ME.
The step up into the train was easy for a little girl.
"I have grown some. Also trains
are more dignified."

Two windows in the caboose projected from the side
of the train, one from each side,
so you could see from one window all the entrances
on one side of the train.
From the other window all the entrances
on the other side.
The railroad was for the the transport of grain,
mostly wheat. But not at this time of year.
There were only two passengers besides Irene.
The pine seats were worn and hard.

After a long time there was a great jolt to start.
"Something has been born."

Think again*

(fantastic riches)

"Weep, weep, weep, weep. Let down your beautiful hair,
Dilectissima, in hot July. Comb out your
auburn hair, Irene, daughter of a leaping deer.
Cover us over." —The peonies say, "Think again."
Birth, in its loneliness, cries, "Think." John comes
back from the Wilderness, bearing fantastic riches,
honey and honeybees, echoing odors of announcement,
and is stopped cold at the threshold of the world.

New poet, think again the infinite poem of repentance,
the mind turned back upon itself, thinking the divine
thought of thought: the ax set to the root of the tree.
The ax says: "Bring forth fruit in THIS season or die."
How to do things with tears? Poet, *new* poet, "creation"
is the birth-smile after ten months (Eclogue 4).
The poem is nothing.
The poet smiles at his mother and says YOU. That's all.

HERE is the threshold of the world, where the mind
is stopped cold. THE SUN THE SUN THE SUN is out to lunch
and a private afternoon with the boy Phaethon.
("More power to them," says Victorious.
"LOGOS is Social Security.") The new poet
smiles, and says HELLO to them all, and thinks,
"This is not my scene but I can get into it."

The stars flee away. They are nothing
to the NEW realist.* The moony moon gone, following
the arrows of her "shining bow" into VOID
leaving a pleasure ground, a pain ground,
with a thread around it. On the earth, on *this* side
of the thread, the grass is brown and beaten down,
disturbed with much passage of feet.

*See "Note 2. Stanzas on poetic realism," p. 94 below.

Not all wanderers are lost

(A leafy elegy)

1.

"Hey YOU! What's the joke?" —In a crowded photograph
a boy is grinning, and looking up, and to his left!
"Wipe that grin off your face, kiddo! This is
the Day of the Dead and over all are shadows."
The boy thought about it for a long time
and in the fluent course of time he grew

to be a beautiful youth. *Then* he answered me.
"Sad old man, do not weep for this philosopher.
do not even remember him. *Remember, instead,*
what he remembered—:THE LUMINOUS BODY
OF TRUTH, a great golden head never shorn,
a white bosom not feminine but promising

abundant sweetness, a genital to be stroked
and sucked and received with gratitude
and all the rest." "*At the end,* when the sky darkens
and night and the shadows are over all,
will there be no thought-storm, no fulgurous

lightning as I turn my face to the wall?"
"No! Only *susurrus* of rain on salt pond,
on garden, and on the forest floor: leaf
over leaf, leaf over leaf, leaf over leaf,
oak over beech and over oak the pine,
and over all the shadows?" —Then, the beautiful

youth, *still* grinning ("SO, kid, what IS the joke?),
lines out a song called "Benefits of Rain"
and everybody in the photo, living and dead,
joins the chorus, first one and then another one.
They sing in turn. But when each song is done
they sing it all, together, again.

2.

—I have found these moments before my death,
which may yet be many or few, in any case
a long schoolroom. There is, for example, a
river in Babylonia called the Over-
flowing River.... *Remember, old man,*
what I remember. Do not remember me.

Then the smirking boy calls out another verse:
"Rain was before all things. In the beginning,
rain was equivalent to the resurrection
when all the dead stand up, as in a picture,
and from the heavens pour down memories,
destroying everything, dragging down the hills

where many keep the room they were born in
and now die. Deep calls to Deep in the voice
of cataracts! And the dead cry their cry, *'Remember*
What I remember. Do not remember me.'"
—It is true, as I now remember, even jewels
benefit from the rain, as do the fields,

the sown and the unsown and the blue thistle.
"Ocean water is water that eats water.
The ocean is *insatiable* of rain.
The entire Name-Of-God is not enough.
BEFORE religion was God. BEFORE God
was holiness. BEFORE holiness was

the sound of waters disappearing under waters:
Land's End—and, then, *Lyoness, Lyoness, Lyoness*".
In the photo, all the dead sing it—*Ly-o-ness.*
The sound of their song is as rain is far out,
rain falling into open ocean at first light,
the TRUE light, without color, making things clear:

In the beginning, the frozen minute of Creation's
photographic flash, lightning-like, portending rain,
Grandpa Harry (up front in the picture), a *Jewish* farmer
(what a laugh!), crushes something, I don't know what,
in his right hand. And there stands Harry-the-farmer's
deaf daughter Dorothy who tutored Tuesday Weld

and died in the bath (of a massive heart attack)
in Sri Lanka on a California teacher's pension.
And next to Dorothy, Aunt Rose, *con de la famille*
who devoured one blossom each morning for breakfast,
smiles to remember what she remembers: how
her CEO fiancé was conked in an ill-considered

jibe and drowned off Sirmione, April 1937.
Dear God! Remember what Rose remembers.
Do not remember her. And there in the back row
Is our Uncle Leo, an Ann Arbor junkman
who still remembers the lost, billion dollar
locomotives he found (Leo, dream on!) rusting

in Wisconsin corn fields (ca. '42). And Bess his hairy-
chested wife who tormented her male children
until at last they ate their dinners off the floor
with the other kitchen filth and died young:
Merton (life insurance) *dead* (cross him off);
Mickey (auto sales) *dead* (cross him off);

and another whose name I can't remember.
Also Uncle Raymond, bus driver, thick as a post
(married to a narrow person with a wan smile,
daughter of the whirlwind traffic of contingency)
who once stopped for me and said, jamming his clutch
with an enormous boot: "YOU'RE ON THE WRONG BUS, BOY."

So THAT'S the joke, kiddo? *"Not all wanderers
are lost."* And who is rabbi? *"He to whom
the people come."* Remember what I remember:
a girl's body of light, as smooth as glass—
Diana, her genital a star.
Remember what I remember. Do not remember me.

I am the gazing ball wherein does congregate
all the light there is. And I am the philosopher
who saw the naked goddess plain (body of truth!).
I am rememberer of the garden oak
in its mysterious well. I am the peony that harbors
in its ear the ant, the worm, the water drop.

I am acquainted with the shouting tiger lily
(I will tell you *everything* it says),
the whispering baby breath, the pansy low,
and in its season the all silencing snow
that fills the well where the oak stands, and stills
the garden and the tongues of all its fires.

At the bottom of the garden, in the waste
where the paths end, grow the RESISTER WEEDS,
makers of the poet's mind (*"remember what I remember"*)—
square root of two. O woe. There the *body* learns
something about the body: WHATEVER IN THAT
WASTE IS ROOTED, THAT THING IT CANNOT MOVE.

To this place the death-animals of Diana
followed me. Where is she NOW? Take ship,
heavy with lights, so burdened that the phosphorescent
ocean paints the deck, leaf over leaf, gold over green.
Land ho! There shines Diana's star on Delos,
There sleeps the goddess with her gruesome animal.

—A man or woman without religion is mad.
His children are mad, and also her children
eat filth and die. RIGHT HERE (*sparagmos*)
in the waste places among RESISTER WEED.
The philosopher turns his face to the wall
at the moment of death. The philosopher remembers

(himself he does not know) what God remembered
in the beginning. The God, before religion,
wept for himself, alone, among the sanctities.
Then the God forgot himself: "LET THE LIGHT BE."
(The Lord, Our God, teaches us how to do things
with tears.) Then, the great God forgot himself.

(THE GOD IS THE SELF THAT FORGETS HIMSELF.)
Then the God forgot himself and remembered LIGHT,
LIGHT that has heaped up in the Roman paths
of Lyoness, under water now, time out of mind,
light that has no colors, *no rainbow at its heart*
under 40 fathoms. The shallow sea is

a hard crossing to the rats and the one palm tree
of the Scilly Isles. This is the Day of the Dead.
But the poet is still working (night falls in the room)
as the light fails, still working in a room
at this leafy elegy. But now it is done.
NOT ALL WANDERERS ARE LOST. NOT EVEN YOU.

"America is the greatest poem, as Whitman said.
In fact, America *is only* a poem. Old man,
here's another joke: the God is many.
But—hear, O Israel!—THE LIGHT IS ONE.
NOW. Shall I tell you my *best* joke? It's a doozer."
—Give me a break, kid. I've heard them all.

PART THREE

DO NOT BE CONTENT WITH AN IMAGINARY GOD

Weird River

We sit down on the rocks above a river
like three Crows in ruin. Star Asper burns
in the pure heaven. The voice of the star
utters *one* law: *You must account for everybody.*
The night is cold and getting colder. Dawn

far away. —Suddenly, the First Crow asks,
"How shall I start?" The burning Star replies,
"Look down. What do you see?" The First Crow says,
"It's cold enough to snow." "You can't *see* cold,"
says the Star. "OK, I see a *girl* washing

a corpse," says Crow One. "Also, a big dog."
—By this time, the other Crows are getting restless.
They want to say something too, but the night wind
is cold and makes a loud sound. —"Was this ruin
ever whole and a flourishing house?"

whispers the Second Crow under his breath.
The burning Star sighs. He can hear small sounds.
"This place was always a ruin, where gather
all souls in flocks toward the wild migration
from life to life in the same world," Star Asper

smiles sadly on the tumult at the dark river.
The Second Crow, having found a hollow
in the ruined wall, quickly falls asleep
and cries in his dreams. Crow Three says, "Look, Star,
one law is too many. I can't do it."

"Then I'll add another law," says Star Asper
in a great voice: *No other book than YOURS!*
—The dog howls at the light. Frightened by the
dog, the three crows fly away. And rosy Dawn
in tears, is heard to say: "Weird river, flow on."

Flora's ABC

(6 Perseid sonnets, meteors of late August)

1.

—At that time I learned to be a coal miner.
We were 20 girls to begin with. One day,
a butcher's daughter from Luxembourg whispered,
"I'm afraid, Flora. *Something's going to happen.*
The SS are saying, 'What your father did
to meat we are going to do to YOU.'
Stay away from me, Flora." She was a day
and a half dying. We stood, compelled to look.
(God gives. And God takes.) —Afterward, we went
back to the mines. Underground, I learned to
speak the language of the dead: *ABC.*
The dead were speaking the language of the dead
to stones. Among the dead was a clean beast
who addressed me with a certain authority:

2.

"This time of year the Perseids return,
prodigal sons of God who have wandered away.
—Lying in the field, among August things,
we see that it is so: this *is* that time
the Perseids go down. They *do*. Southwest,
Northeast. Flame out and disappear. The Perseids
are coming to be and passing away.
But why are you weeping, Flora?" I weep
on account of the beauty that is going
to rot in earth. "On that account," she said,
"surely you have reason to weep." We both wept.
Then, she turned toward me. And I recognized
the voice and eye. "Living or dead," she whispered,
"do not be content with an imaginary God."

3.

August already. August everywhere.
The Perseids are coming to be all night
and passing away. In ever-weeping
Baltimore, we do not sleep. But go forth
on the Western mountains, with timbrels, singing,
miraculously 19 sisters still
(we were 20 but one rots in earth).
This is the material Sabbath,
our reprieve. But winter is at the door.
Winters we resume our Work among the stones,
dragging coal through tunnels to the port.
Also we milk the soul-cows and sell the cream.
Our god, our God, the real McCoy—say it
in Dead, philosopher—is ADONAI.

4.

I love the field, and others of my generation
love the field: how it rises gently toward
its center, for good drainage; how mowing it
does not prevent encroachment of young trees
that will soon enough make a small forest
darkening earth, so that the Lady's Bedstraw
and the Blackberry, the Milkweed, and clover
cannot live; how the path the children make
on their six-day journey into the world
has disappeared because they're now grown up;
how the grass is lodged where the beasts sleep.
Here patience does its perfect work—a field:
this is Flora's ABC, material Sabbath,
a clearing in space open to the stars.

5

How admirable that the body bears the
soul! How admirable the soul *does live*
and looks about! —Therefore, weep! that the body
must wander—tormented by strangers—by death
disgraced! *Just so* the Ark of the Lord, harnessed
to milk cows by the Philistine police,
was dragged (O radiant waste! too hot to handle!)
until it foundered in that low wet pasture
where all roads run in (I Sam. 6): a wheel
cracked, then shattered. Unbalanced by the giddy
weight of Nothing inside, the Ark was wrecked.
The soul-cows mired at the bottom of the field.
And down among the golden mice and emeralds
ens realissimum in the shit lies dead.

6

Then the butcher's daughter from Luxembourg
spoke again in her language. "What *do* I know?
A plow rusts in the field. The field is the
common world. How admirable! To that place
all roads run in among the mice and emeralds,
the nothing. There lies the *ens realissimum*
in earth. An eating rust feeds on the mists.
Beware the sex of young men without education.
Such sex desires the death of women. Flora,
do not be content to say 'YAHWEH LORD.'
Say rather 'Her father was butcher in Luxembourg.'
Do not be content to say, 'Lady's Bedstraw'.
Say, 'Her virginity.' Do not say, *'Creator spiritus
veni.'* Say 'Windflower' or, maybe, 'Anemone.'

SHAZAM!

1.

April noon. A man is reading in his garden.
The garden has been ruined by an unseasonable
snowstorm. He looks up from his book and watches
the textile shadows weaving and unweaving
darkness and light. He remembers his night dreams
that foretold the heart attack from which
he is recovering. The man has been reading
Sir Walter Ralegh's HISTORY OF THE WORLD
open before him at the last page: "Eloquent,
just and mightie Death. . . ." —He talks to an
absent friend as if she were present: "*Dilectissima,*

2.

the sliding shadows of the oak above me
move easily over the leaf-strewn earth below
without a sound. Such as they are, they will be—:
filmy, watery, wind-flung nylons, night-fishing
punctually at noon—night in day, day
altogether light, a moment in a garden
strewn with leaves, covered with winter trash.
On the gray trunks of the pine trees the shadows
of oak leaves glide over a dish of water
visited by pictures of sparrows in need of a wash,
also the looming oak, the blown sky, the golden sun.

'I am El Dorado's voice, sexual brooder,
who says, "LIGHT!"' At the beginning, the sun rises
outside the window, extinguishing the beacons.
(If *you* cannot hear that voice, you nonetheless
know there is such a voice. And you imagine
what it says:—'Something happened TO ME.')
I am the Golden Man of whom they whisper:
'In the hour before dawn, dust of gold
is applied to his body with spoons. When
the rising sun strikes his thigh—POW! DoRAdo!—,
The salute is redoubled in the heavens.'

4.

And Light (a solitary weeper on windy roads,
dawdler in the darkest hour, the hour
before the dawn) builds up the LIGHT ORATION,
one note and then another one, and staggers
like a squall in this direction, across
the bright lake (from nothing to something), darkening
the water, waking the boats. —What DOES it say?
WHAT, Dorado? . . . Look! Through the east window!
The sun is hoisting up a gilded body:
half-hanged, genitals cut out and burned—quartered
and impaled on the four gates of the city.

5.

So *you* tell me, *dilectissima*, what kind
of knowledge is this premonitory dream?
I woke up. I heard you whispering to someone
up there: 'He's not alive, nor is he dead.'
That's true, beLIEVE ME (I thought). It could
go either way . . . When are you coming home?
. . . In any case, *I must keep where I am*
or I'll blunder into death by mistake
before you come. Though God is letting roll
a great pain on me, I'll stay where I am.
But come quickly, kid. You will not meet me

6.

anywhere else.' —That's what I thought. Then pain
did thunder down on me, as the dream said.
The God, in fact, let roll great pain out of
his hill. And that has brought me close to death.
BUT I'M STILL HERE. I write it one last time:
If I don't love YOU. I love no one on earth.
Maybe it *is* all letters, kid:—*epistolae*
from the Gates of Ivory. But now, once more, impatient
to hear the truth, they crowd the threshold at dawn,
insolent children in conspicuous clothes.
'Tell us (they shout) the premonitory dream'—:

7.

'I'm on the train with rattan seats once more.
No honey-blond Fate this time. No kisses, Hard
Winter on the Great Plains of dream. In the caboose
the cast iron stove is cold. It repeats:
'If I am good, tell others about me.'
The rest is silence. The windows of the train
are crowded with papery faces staring in.
Behind them are many immaculate houses
where the light of Star Asper falls the same
in every room. Consider, kid! Unutterable
pain assures us of our perfect conviction

8.

That what we know is TRUE! —Look about you!
This town is home, ELOQUENT DEATH, Minnesota,
last stop in space and time. An April snow
rises in the cold air. On the gleaming rail
the departing train is leaning on a curve.
What do I hear? High up, in empty heaven
where the lark was, someone is saying out loud:
'His crime was trafficking in light. High treason.
But this is his old age—nocturnal foldedness
of day on day, *floral*. When light diminishes,
the flower withdraws into itself. Then

9.

leaf upon leaf faces a sister, and recites
all night her history by the light of kindred
faces until dawn extinguishes the beacons
and the golden voice is without assurance.'
Therefore, you visible and invisible agents
who produce the days—this day and another one—
I have nothing beautiful to say to you.
In a night, pain has changed the voice of
Eldorado. I hear the fatal whisperers:
'Take the wings of morning (they say) and dwell
in the farthest chambers of the east.' *Come*

10.

quickly, *dilectissima!* It is all too clear.
I'm adrift in a garden of bright shadow.
Star Asper burns in the heavens. By day, I read
the last words of THE HISTORY OF THE WORLD:
'My harp also is tuned to mourning. . . . '
By night, I search for you the whole length
of the longest rivers: Mississippi, Oronoco
(kid, you went away to a wedding dressed up
like a wedding guest and never came back)
and the endless Okeanos which flows
around all things. In the river cities,

11.

the ringing of consecrated bells, echoing
in sleep, averts the hurricane and the tornado.
But gravity, eloquent as death, conducts
the patient river to the gulf, bearing with it,
like granite on a barge, the voice of El Dorado
who says out loud: 'Something happened to ME.
EVERYTHING moves in the April garden.
Like an extinguished flame or a lost water,
THE VOCATION IS REVOKED. Rivers flow on
without the light of heaven or of earth.
In vain do rivers run. . . . ' —I hear nothing

12.

but the whisperers: 'When he acknowledged (finally)
that he was incurably ill, his logic forced
him to realize *also* that he would cease
to exist and *hence cease to have thoughts.*
Yet this is a conclusion the full content
of which is incomprehensible to the human
intellect and therefore horrified him.
It was heartbreaking to watch the frustration
of his mind, when all hope was gone, in its
struggle with the fate it knew to be
unavoidable yet *unacceptable.*'

13.

—Today, at the remembered daily session
before the dawn, the perennial shadowless
season, when the nocturnal cats, net-fishers all,
cry out in the garden at the pictured birds,
each one a word of power, come for a wash
in the dish. Seated at the east window on
the bed's edge at the darkest hour of the garden,
the punctual moment of the extinguishing
of the beacon, SUDDENLY I SAW SHAZAM!
our late Minister of Public Works,
at his table in the Town Offices (second

14.

floor) of ELOQUENT DEATH, Minnesota through
which town the railroad runs. As I remember him,
a man of indeterminate age with vertical
creases in his face that run from his jaw
to his hairline. A dusty green bird of treasonous
mind is under foot. The bird eats SHAZAM'S ms.,
scalloping them page after page. A big book
is a grand meal for a green bird. I said:
'SHAZAM!'(what else?). He said: 'Whatever is
it's all in the light. POW! All shine, Dorado.'
I thought: This place, in Minnesota, is

15.

the navel of the dream, the first stop in time,
ELOQUENT DEATH. The next towns on are: NECESSITY,
SILENCE, OBLIVION, and (just east of FARGO) TRUTH.
Before I could open my mouth SHAZAM!
SPEAKS AGAIN: 'Shut up FOR HEAVENS SAKE! I'll send
a guy out to your house with a rake to repair
your garden (a Public Work?).' —I heard, then,
sounds of a wedding in another room
where women sang (the Death Watch Group): 'Domestic
gaiety, pregnancy, mourning, committee work
and spoons in the drawer that do not match.'

16.

—First light. *Dilectissima*, I am heartened
by your daily return. (We say, strangely,
'I *think* she has entered the room.') Isn't it
for that you came back at last from the wedding,
stepped out of your clothes, your gold and your shine,
naked in front of everyone except
for your shameless nylons' slithery shade,
and went for a walk on the garden path
throwing up your lilac fingers in despair
to see the garden as it is, that you
left so fine? Noon now. The gold all gone."

17.

The man closes his book and rises up.
I hear him say, "Death is nothing to be feared."
And, then, he says the same sentence again,
"Death is nothing to be feared. . . ." —Someone or other
is moving in the garden, raking out the beds.
The wind weaves or unweaves the shadowy veil
of naked April. There comes to mind another
dream and other histories. But *this* masterless
man, the golden slave, opens his throat:
"Spare me," he says, "that I may recover strength
before I go away and be no more."

Reason for eating pig

"Why do you ask my name, seeing it is Wonderful!
I am the Judensau, irresistible."

—"Up out of the intricated branches of
the nest of sleep, like the last song of
a songbird who pronounces one human word
after an immeasurable lapse of not saying
anything but warble from the beginning
of time. But now the *word* which is the meaning
of all song comes to mind in the hour
before dawn, a whispered but unmistakable *word*.
The very song of very song, at the end
of the world, arises thread-like out of
the nest of sleep in the summer of song.
I see now things are not as I once thought.
This hour, this minute, this second of no return
will never come again—never never never."

"Eat me, Jew. Eat me. And you will not die."

Latch

(bespoke coffin-maker in purgatory)

Only God can make a tree

"THIS GROVE LACKS AN ALTAR." —So Latch built
A temple and an altar.

Templum aedificavit.
How shall I remember the use of his tools?

(A coffin-maker among the Immortals.
What a scream!)

　　　　　　—Where *is* that Latch now?
Will I see him again in his shadowy cave
on this purgatorial mountain of memory?
And the other immortal hosts: John Skermo,
the gardener; Mary Snorak, the fat cook
in her great sack (500 lbs.); and lonesome Jack
the parts-man who loves her and can take a joke?

In the far dark, at the back of Latch's shop,
against a rock wall, is the turning-lathe
which Latch powers by hand, Egyptian fashion.
With a strung bow, Latch makes knops and flowers—
as it is written (Exodus 25): "A knop and a flower."
On the living rock above his gigantic
lathe there shines, bright from sharpening and use,
a graded series of knives. For sure, kid!

Latch is one guy who KNOWS THE USE OF TOOLS!
(A gentile—to be frank.) How shall *I* remember?
Latch says: "IF A TEMPLE IS TO BE ERECTED,
A TEMPLE MUST FIRST BE DESTROYED. . . . "
(All this writing follows from that.)

"Then, do not rebuild it!" says Skermo, the gardener.
"The whole idea of Justice has taken
a wrong turn," he goes on, "no longer sacralizing
Justice as such, nor truth, but PAIN. Only God"
concludes the carpenter, "can make a tree."

"Then do not rebuild it!" says Mary Snorak, the cook.
"That there is a Hell does not surprise me;
but that Justice made it is beyond belief."
Then Mary Snorak exits sidewise for a smoke
under a tree and Jack dies laughing again.

DO NOT REBUILD IT!—by the waters of
the Mississippi where it flows past Babylon,
under the burdened willows that are there,
Latch was a mystery. And (as I thought)
"Aphrodite is in his bed." Latch limped.
"Aphrodite must like men who limp," I surmised.
So I learned to limp.

         —What's Latch making now,
our only coffin-maker on the mountain?
(A year or two ago—not long!—I began to SEE
DISTINCTLY a common world, the meaning of all song,
as when on an island mountain, high above
the *Wunderkammer* of ocean, the night wind
shifts offshore in the hour before dawn and
the night air, *dilectissima,* brightens and clears.)
Among shadows, at his lathe, Latch is not sad.
Ingenious cripple with a trophy wife,
he is still the sole source, in the afterlife,
of knops and flowers for the mortuary trade.

A Grand Caprice

In a Grand Caprice, cream, top of the line
with a real good ride, hands feet and air,
a legacy—memorial of Louis, *maître de penser*
of Minneapolis—I depart the Cities, where
I was thrown, southward to a town fragile, worn
thin as a bottom sheet, Enigma MN.

. . . What *is* this apparition? The weirdest structure
known: Town Hall, Enigma MN. LOCKED.
Upstairs, "Messiah" (the piano) fascinates ladies.
Ground floor, the registry of true-love kisses.
Who's there? The ghost of a good man. *Dead.*
Who else? The ghost of a good woman. *Dead.*

She sings, "My friend is he who, at the same time,
is and is not. To him I am a friend
who, at the same time, am and am not.
I'm a faithful friend to him and he is
a faithful friend to me, forever and a day.
Hand and hand, we walk appearing and disappearing

until the end. Then we sing Leadbelly's song
"Goodnight, Irene. I'll see you in my dreams."
There's no world other than this common world,
no pain, no joy other than this pain or joy."
He: "But let me look." *She*: "I'll let you look."
He: "I myself, as a myth, step forth to marry you,

yourself as a truth. Do you, as a truth,
take me *as I am*, a myth, to the end that
out of our union will be born once more
real children, and the OLD MURDER of everyone
continue as before, the children waste and
in Death's arms die." *She*: "The least part of a day

is eternal life. In your arms appearing
and disappearing I am *completely happy."*
He: "The world comes to mind dark, silver, quick."
She: "The world comes to mind dark, silver, quick.
At the dark end of the day, the blinded second
is enough. —In my dreams, will you answer

one question?" "What is your question my dear?"
"Where have you gone? Country and town are empty
of you. Post office, airport, telephone exchange
and all the high and hidden places are empty
of you and I have taken refuge in my dream
of the incomprehensible Town Hall, Enigma, MN.

There is nothing here but snow. And the crows
calling, 'What for?', 'In vain', 'Nothing.' The Sioux
are at the door of my dream. LOCKED. Mayakovsky's
ghost at the piano fascinates the ladies:
'Get it straight, sweet hearts! Religions are
systems of cruelty and also *all* social arrangements.'

Who's there? The ghost of a good man. *Dead.*
Who's there? The ghost of a good woman. *Dead.*
There is nothing here but snow." —"Take this kiss.
O my truth, do not try to remember me. Remember
instead the dark myth left empty at my death,
staining the worn bottom sheet, fragile, and thin.

Open the registry, Registrar! Write down this kiss.
The snow is filling the great plains of the dream.
The rivers stop their flow, the paths are nowhere.
Quick! Come away with me, Irene. Take a spin
in the cream. Do not remember me. Remember
instead my grand machine. Come away with me,

Your left hand on my mythy knee, my right
hand groping your truth. Pedal to the metal,
engine hitting on 8, windows down,
leather smelling good, Enigma fading fast.
(Bye bye, Town Hall!) Come away, O beautiful youth!
Our Grand Caprice, top of the line, drifts South.

Thunderstruck

Hey kid! Sex and the death of men bring tourists
from near and far. Not monuments or reverent
deeds but the predation of wild dogs,
the sex dogs and the death dogs which are gods.

Egypt! Egypt! Of your reverent deeds
only stories will survive. And they will
be incredible to your children. —Nonetheless,
I, who am *fulminato* (thunderstruck), write out

how it is (believe *me*) I've two bad hats:
—August, in Egypt, a majestic day.
Thunderous. What fell to earth? and why?
What traffic in the air? What Grand Caprice

along the ground blew off my hat that settled
in the stream—like Cowper's "Castaway,"
and vanished from the eye? In the *same* instant
I saw the bloody animal on the rail.

WHAT DOG KILLED THIS CAT? —Summer lies on the horse's
face like a hood of flies, covering the nostrils
and the eyes. Spring bleats still from over there
under the hill, like unseen sheep. The bull,

no slouch, is hard at work among the dampish
rot of bottom amaranth. And the badger
from the badger's set is out. The dead cat
welters in its blood. And the hat is lost.

O kid! What is the interest of all this?
What, then, shall we love? I am thunderstruck
like an old man who suddenly remembers
he has killed his own son, drunk on the roads.

Here come the tourists forsaking the pyramids
to look at *me*. I'm sick to death of the light
by which I live. You and I know, *dilectissima*,
the agile dog Anubis hunts the beautiful

foals of the wild mares on the dike above
the town. He says, "Sex is better than death
although not so easy to come by." —And now
it dawns on me: that's what is called TRUE-LOVE.

Keep your distance, kid. I'm a dangerous man.
Lightning follows me. Whoever built the pyramids
did it in *one day*. —Lightning follows me
and then thunder and—soon enough—the rain.

X-rated

Slowly, slowly run, you horses of the night

OK. In the Vatican Museum I
am looking at the pictures (and the rest of
it)—with a tidal bore of Jews and poets
(like me) thundering in. —Suddenly, I see
a naked satyr's beautiful legs, etc.

out for a walk, a child on his lissom breast:
an unfinished thing, asleep in its principle
or just awakened, arms flung out and up
toward the face of the satyr who holds him
with laughter and infinite grace and sweetness

and looks intently into his face without
reserve and says out loud, "I am your true-love."
Consider this, dear, how much more beautiful
the *unfinished* stair. Birdlike it takes wing
at the crack of dawn and is long gone

before the glory empties out and scatters in
the brightening air. As it was in the beginning,
between the God's thought of light and his saying
of it, unspeakable beauty in that unborn
word—the bright all—light no longer chaos—

firmament, not yet—before the saying of it
wrecked the principle of its being here
(even the light!). What are the golden builders
doing in mournful, ever-weeping Baltimore
now the masons have come in their soft hats

and the helmeted riggers are long gone?
Don't touch me, kid. Say nothing. These are cheap
seats—right field—for an illegal night game.
Soon. Soon the sun will rise and will devour
the god's spectacular white ear of corn.

Your laughing lover

As you came from the holy land
Of Walsingham,
Met you not with my true-love
By the way as you came?

Yes. As I came from the Holy Land, among
men of the roads, I met your true-love walking.
She said to me: "Everyone wants to KNOW."
She'd tied something about her leg which weighed
her down and hindered her walk. A long road
it was from the Holy Land with this hindered

walking in winter weather beside yowling
streams. For it had been raining cats and dogs
in the Holy Land out of the open sky
and the West was filled with bodies draining
on that torrent from the East. Your true-love
fished out one dead cat and wears the corpse

under her dress, which thing hinders, as I
said, her walking. It makes your true-love laugh
out loud because everyone wants to know
what she has under her dress. "That's what,"
she says, "everyone wants to know." I can tell *you*
it's a dead cat. *True-love makes strange sex.*

I can tell YOU also that your laughing lover
is still yours and doesn't forget. So tie
her big word in *your* groin. Take it from me:
the sun, the moon, the heavens, and the earth
are common, the torrent beside the road
and the voice of it, the laughter of water.

Take it from me. That burden is *your true-love's*
child lugged from the Holy Land among men
of the roads, through a long life of hindered walking.
I have been gone a long time and am back,
no longer an able man. But I've something
to tell you everyone wants to know.

—What heaps up? Of what material is
the trace of age in mind? Of what substance
that knowledge? I have come back from the Holy
Land an old man with sore feet, etc.,
bearing home, yowling, your true-love's child—
such trouble to carry, such hindered walking,

such waste of time under the open sky
in that winter weather! Death is a waste
of space and time, a waste of rain and snow,
a waste of this very snow that falls night-long
and at first light falls still, until all roads,
our first road and our last, are lost.

Crow

A crow flapped its wings like a halcyon
and settled on a jutting rock.
A long wave engulfed the rock.
The crow-halcyon flew up and disappeared.
The wave continued toward the shore.

The wave raised itself again, climbed
the edge of ocean.
Then it said its say: "You will die
by the hands of Crow."
"But crows don't have hands." "In that case,"
said the wave, "you won't die."

The wave was a long wave. When it finished its
say it did not stop but sang a song,
with battles in it and sighs. Then I
heard a short cry, a sharp sound, and the Ocean
pouring like a waterfall.

I lifted up my eyes. Lo and behold! The Death
ship, DANMARK, towing up wind
toward harbor, Copenhagen, out of sight. And
the halcyon, on broken ramparts of water,
crow-wings black as anthracite,
folding capable hands.

Star Asper

Sunrise. The star Asper.
Sunset. The star Hesper.
Something is coming
to pass without me

I was born to see.
What you see is your duty
to say, forever.
When you are young

things go by fast
seen from the train
a mile a minute
on the Milwaukee Road.

High up, love and war.
The Queen of the slopes
processes with her animals.
Omnia vincit amor.

Now I am old
things go by like lightning,
—I have no doubt
what I see. *Da steht*

Der Todt! Black salt.
First the star Asper, *Amor,*
before dawn, arose.
Then the star Hesper. *Mors.*

The train runs on
to Chicago.
But the river
low, down

Egyptian
father continues
(I see it)
to ocean.

PART FOUR

THREE NOTES ON COMMON CONCERNS UNDER STAR ASPER

*Note 1. Stanzas on pots. On pots in general and three imag-
ined instances of pot, illustrating conscious body as in
"WHITE SAILS."*

The meaning of Irene's pot (p. 34 above), and a secret of all pots, is
the testimony of pot to humankind's momentary triumph, body and
mind, over the (fatal) leakiness of things. Such triumph may be sim-
ple and effectual (as in ceramic plainware), or may be at the same
time effectual and celebratory (high fashion artifacts, like poems).

Mind is a pot ("crazed" is broken), body is a pot (may it not leak, the
beautiful body full of assurance), the biological cell is a pot (filled
full), song is a pot (full of our meaning, almost unbreakable). Pots are
memory-stores (the Greeks stored almost everything in pot form,
especially stories of greatest and simplest possibility and the traces of
persons, the "dark myth"). The oldest text in the human world is
"face"—the inscribed ornament of the skull pot. The lamp is a skull
pot and, when shattered, "the light in the dust lies dead."

a. A plainware cup, Japanese or Chinese like Irene's, blue-green,
high-fired (in a technologically advanced kiln) makes a theatrical
show of difference between inner and outer, without which differ-
ence *we cannot keep* anything—the surface shows the melt from which
pot rescues us moment to moment. This one fits the hand but is
slightly larger than need, therefore contributes consciousness of pot
among its uses.

b. A flared low-fired (less advanced technology) red clay jar theatri-
calizes balance/off-balance, i.e. keeping/spilling, continually losing
and recovering function before your eyes—a show pot that tells the
general pot story necessary to life and also *keeps* water necessary to
life.

c. Everyone has seen in the museum great north China paleolithic
pots with four eyes. A death pot (of this kind there are thousands
buried with the dead who need a pot to piss in worse than us). Urn
burial. It re-presents and re-minds of mind prior to consciousness,
and it holds on to conscious mind even when life is gone.

*

Note 2. Stanzas on poetic realism. Some propositions under Star Asper.

a. "Poetry" is the most general theory of assemblage. Poetry may be poems, or may be something else. But poems, to be *good enough to care for, must present to mind new knowledge.* More precisely must *present to conscious mind* such knowledge as consciousness already is burdened with, and decide what is important and what is not. New poetry must compel acknowledgement of what mind knows, and deliver, in practice, *a new poetic realism.* Otherwise it can be of no interest, or worse, a waste of attention.

Star Asper thinks about thinking, hears very small sounds, and rewards sedition.

b. The poet, daughter of the shark (p. 35 above), opposes the satisfaction of supposing that thinking is innocent, or that it discovers truth only at the moment of reconciliation. Under such delusive circumstances there can be no new knowledge, no poetry.

c. The conviction of sufficient response ("what will suffice," "answerable voice," "closure") is peculiarly delusive. Such conviction misplaces the authority of poetry. Any NEW poetry must be aware that there is nothing that will suffice. Any new poetry must be aware of insufficiency, unanswerability in response to what anybody knows, with respect to what consciousness is conscious of. There is, in this matter of poetic thinking (poetic realism), no distinction possible to be made between consciousness and moral consciousness.

Poetry (the poetic principle) makes no epistemological claims and knows nothing about existence or inexistence. Its concerns are with significance. ("Deliver us / Zion, from mist," p. 4 above). In that sense poetry is anthropo-logic. In order to reconstruct significance, it must consider what is in fact thought. What is thought, what *can* come to mind, figures the world, and determines what in the world *can come to mind.* And can become so intensely interesting. Interest signifies.

d. But the doctrine of what is thought, what *can* come to mind, is under stress. Among those stresses is the (vestigial but potent) requirement of sufficiency, satisfaction, answerability, closure, all which are symptomatic of the refusal of the common world. Closure shuts out interest as does beauty.

What constitutes the common world by which existence is figured or not at all and significance founded? Among other recognitions: the unavoidable awareness of the vast, energetic, punctuated, but unbounded temporal purview of time, time before time, time without time, time after time. Quite new. Also the spatial purview of the whole universe which has no universal characteristics, no boundary, no closure. Quite new. The purview, also, of the irreducible claims of the universality of consciousness, *that well of tears*. All minds are now conscious and make equally valid claims. Any new poetry must be aware that nothing can suffice. It is not that there is no witnessing but that the only witnesses are the dead. Delusional sufficiency of (the artistic form of) speaking (that "sabbath of the will") is the old way and cannot warrant confidence. The torturer is more confident of the universality of pain than the poet.

e. The true poet says: "I DO the best I can. I also *KNOW* better." And assuredly knowing better IS closer to poetry than the "poem" and more justifiably convincing. Poetry is constituted, invariably, as an account of conscious life and must be adequate to what consciousness takes in. Otherwise, the best of it is good for nothing. There's plenty of nothing without art.

f. At the bottom of conscious life is the knowledge (consciousness itself) of consciousness' dependence on another nature that is not itself. "The navel of the dream." At the navel of the dream interpretation stops, because just THERE consciousness disappears into the organic brain which knows nothing. At the moment of this point of appearance /disappearance, creation (in every mind, in every trade, in every culture) constructs itself. Creativity, the poetic principle, is stationed at that point, guards the navel of the dream, the beginning and the end of significance. Action on this limit (this "threshold of the world" which stops thought cold [p. 30 above]) is creation whether by God or Man—the poetic principle. Shelley calls it "poetry in the general sense," the general theory of assemblage, sexual, political, or artifactual: of which the MOST general instance is the zero probable union and reciprocal contingence of mind and body.

g. Once again: the poem is not as close as you can get to THE POET-IC PRINCIPLE. And that is what we are after. Call it Poetic realism, the shark attack. Even if there were (even if there are, strictly speaking) no poems (there *are, strictly speaking, no poems*) there is still poetry—the principle which makes the common world (the inter-subjective, inter-personal world *so far as it goes*.)

h. Plato, profoundly, resented the superior authority of poetry. About the absurdity of poets he was right. About the inevitable superiority of the anthropo-logic text—he was also right. But he could not endure its powerlessness. Hence, Socrates.

i. The poem is not the poetry. Telling about thinking about thinking is more like it. Aristotle or (Irene) on God's thought ("The Kiss-stone of the Fate," p. 37 above). And thinking about thinking is always thinking at that limit ("navel of the dream") from which consciousness arose and into which it will die "when the lamp is shattered." Consider the 12th stanza of "SHAZAM!" (p. 74 above). John von Neumann faces death:

> 'When he acknowledged (finally)
> that he was incurably ill, his logic forced
> him to realize *also* that he would cease
> to exist and *hence cease to have thoughts.*
> Yet this is a conclusion the full content
> of which is incomprehensible to the human
> intellect and therefore horrified him.
> It was heartbreaking to watch the frustration
> of his mind, when all hope was gone, in its
> struggle with the fate it knew to be
> unavoidable yet *unacceptable.*'

j. The poetic principle is the principle of all principles of assemblage—the root contradiction which the Aristotelian Laws of thought cover over (but cf. Heraclitus, or Hegel in the Logic, on contradiction). The "Solitary Reaper" is only a poem. But the solitary reaper is poetry. Irene. "Can no one tell me what she sings?"

What's new NOW? Poetic realism—the poem of the morning star Asper, another hard look.

k. Poetic realism is always, always the will which resists the *imaginary God*, Kant's darling. "Do not be satisfied with an imaginary God." (That is "Flora's ABC," p. 66 above.) An imaginary God is the one God of reconciliation, the inferno, the holy war. But nothing will suffice. An imaginary God is Kant's darling regulative idea. And Nietzsche's. Etc.

l. Novelty (poetic knowledge) is not in the SHAPE of the poem. "Form" is utterly uninteresting. Truth, shape, or "make" lies elsewhere. In the performance of performance. Undeception.

m. Poems are put to use in view of constitutive human bad luck—expressed by pain and death. And, before death, in view of the social or economic deformity of birth in a particular lucky or unlucky place or body (*any* body), in view of scarcity of good things, money, honor, truthfulness. The scarcity of life (mortality). The scarcity of significance which is the *occasion* of the Poetic Principle (radical contradiction, the zero probability of consciousness or Creation).

Poetic thinking is quasi-rational. The figure of poetic thinking ("*What these poems undertake to do*," p. xii above) is the *Sprachweg* (the "word way" or, in fact, counter-logical principle of continuation) from natality, the accident of situated body, all the way to the Cities of significance (the Irene bus trip of conscious experience) and back.

Our late modernism intentionally picks out the poets of constitutive bad luck, mortal "thrown-ness" (e.g., Keats, Lautreamont, Rimbaud, Trakl, Crane, Celan) whose gifts contradict ideas of giftedness, poets who are gifted and given nothing. Not at all the incidental bad luck expressed as rain on one's picnic. Not at all the motivated misconstruction perpetrated and then revoked by the grand comedians of theoretical discourse, i.e., that poetry is the *other* thing to thinking. Whereas, poetic thinking is the thinking without which thinking fails of significance.

n. Poetry is not revolution. It is sedition, origin of thought, light of mind, the lighting up of mind.

> Thou returnst from flight seditious angel
> To receive thy merited reward.
>
> Milton, *Paradise Lost*

*

Note 3. This book is dedicated to the memory of Ilona Karmel Zucker

Shortly before her death (November 2, 2000) Ilona Karmel Zucker, a novelist and teacher, dictated a letter to the New York *Times*. She had seen, in a review of a book by Omer Bartov, "a photograph of the monument on the side of the Krakow-Plaszow concentration camp. The Hebrew inscription, 'Avenge the spilled blood,' is followed by the Polish: 'Here were murdered ten thousand Polish and Hungarian Jews whose names are unknown.'"

To this inscription she responds (in part):

"The names are known; they live in the memory of the former inmates of the camp (of whom I am one). Yet instead of listing the names, I will speak of one known to me not by his name but by his deed—a rabbi chosen to die in a 'selection' of old people conducted on the orders of camp commandant Amon Goeth by members of the Jewish camp police. When they reached the site of execution—the top of a steep hill—the policeman charged with carrying out the order begged the rabbi's forgiveness. He granted it. He then asked for a moment's time. They agreed. The rabbi turned, looked toward the camp—a place where despair turned to sordid vice—reached out his hands in blessing, and said, 'How good are your tents, Jacob, your tabernacle, Israel.'

"Not knowing is often not wanting to know; it is easier to deal with victims than with concrete human beings who once lived a life and bore a name . . . . "